Lake Front

At The Edge of Nature and Nostalgia

Amanda McCallister

LAKE FRONT

AT THE EDGE OF NATURE AND NOSTALGIA

AMANDA MCCALLISTER

ISBN: 9798330555963 (Paperback)
ISBN: 9798330556014 (Hardcover)

Library of Congress Control Number: 2025900804

Front cover image by Amanda McCallister

Printed by Hane Lake Press, in the United States of America.

First printing edition 2025.

Hane Lake Press
1300 3rd ST SW
Suite 182
Winter Haven, FL 33881

www.hanelakepress.com

TABLE OF CONTENTS

ACKNOWLEDGEMENTS

Dad, thank you for the endless boat tours and for your patience, circling those cypress trees time and again until I finally got the shot I was chasing. Thank you for braving the mosquitos to get me close to the nightlife scenes, and for understanding when I took my time, even if it meant annoying a few fellow boaters along the way. I can't wait to make more of these memories.

Mom, thank you for always believing in my wild ideas, no matter how impractical they seemed, and for being my constant cheerleader as I chased every crazy dream. Thank you for always meaning it when you said, "Tell me how I can help," no matter how far you had to drive, how tough the task, or how much spray painting was involved.

Thomas, thank you for letting me chase my dreams down every rabbit hole, even when they disrupted our lives or came with unexpected costs. Thank you for picking up extra responsibilities at home when I got overwhelmed by some self-imposed deadline or detail that, in the grand scheme, might not have mattered all that much. Thank you for always helping me figure out how to make it work and how to get through it.

Yoshi, thank you for being my rock, for standing by me through every anxiety-driven moment, for slowing me down when I needed it, and for feeding me when I forgot to take care of myself. Thank you for keeping promises, big and small, and for making me believe that I am a real artist. Your support taught me how to be an artist and gallerist when opportunities came my way, even when I didn't believe I was ready for them. You know the numbers.

Sherry, thank you for your unwavering leadership, guidance, and wisdom. I've learned so much from you—how to focus on the details without forgetting the big picture, win as the underdog, and make the impossible happen. You've shown me the value of doing the best work I can without expecting appreciation or credit, because that's not why we show up anyways. Your belief in me has been a cornerstone of my journey, and for that, I am forever grateful.

Tina, thank you for letting me chase an opportunity you knew was right for me, and for being my biggest hype woman at every event since. You pushed me out of the nest, and I'm so grateful you did.

Andrew, thank you for opening not just one, but three professional doors for me. Thank you for not accepting my resignation and for your patience when I needed it most. Most of all, thank you for saying my name in rooms where decisions were being made.

Diana, thank you for helping me see what was in the cards, and for your guidance when I needed it.

And to my many aunts, uncles, cousins, and grandparents, thank you for the memories, lessons, and love that inspired this book. Your stories, laughter, and wisdom are the heartbeat behind these pages.

Living in Cypress Shadows

CYPRESS SHADOWS

Beneath their quiet canopy, the cypress bend,
Silent as secrets sinking into soil,
Unyielding guardians through wind and rain,
Absorbing the storms, the sun, the slow churn of seasons.
Their roots reach deep, like fingers tracing buried stories,
And their branches whisper in the wind's old tongue.
They rise, they fall, but they do not break,
Always looking forward to the next hundred years,
Each ring in their bark a silent testament—
Holding the weight of what we've forgotten.
And when twilight tints the sky, they stand,
Like shadows of what remains unsaid,
Sentinels of a time beyond our reach.

Chapter Page: Stranded on an Island. A calm passage framed by towering cypress and palms leads to Lake Summit, reflecting the tension between wilderness and civilization. Here, even in quiet waters, the sense of isolation lingers—an island in the heart of the lakes, where nature holds you still, just long enough to make you wonder how long you've been drifting.

Photo Page: Alone. A solitary figure standing against the elements, this lone cypress is a reminder of the resilience required to endure life on the lakes. Stripped of its companions, it faces the open water and the sky, silently reflecting the strength found in solitude.

Living in Cypress Shadows marks the beginning of a journey, one that is as much about memory as it is about place. For me, that place has always been Winter Haven's Chain of Lakes—a sanctuary of water and time, where the cypress trees stand as enduring sentinels, whispering stories through the rustle of their leaves. The name Cypress Shadows carries a special resonance for me, evoking memories of my days as an editor for a literary magazine at Winter Haven High School, a time when I first began to see the power of words and images to preserve what might otherwise be lost to time. Growing up, the lakes shaped my childhood on Lake Conine, Lake Cannon, and Lake Hartridge, leaving impressions that would never fade. My parents, lifelong lovers of the lakes, introduced me early to this watery world, pulling me along on a kneeboard before I had even outgrown my water wings. Those days, the sun seemed endless, and the lakes felt like they could hold everything.

After graduating from Winter Haven High School in 1998, I pursued a degree in English at Stetson University, where my love for photography and the darkroom blossomed, alongside my relationship with my husband, Thomas. Photography became a way for me to capture those fleeting moments that seemed to slip away too quickly, a way to cheat time and preserve the essence of a place that had always felt eternal. In 2010, I earned a master's degree in Curriculum Design from the American College of Education, expanding my professional reach in education, but my heart remained rooted in photographing Winter Haven and the lakes that had shaped my youth.

The idea for this book began to take shape during the creation of the Lake Front Photography Exhibition with Tree Swallow Gallery. As I curated images of cypress trees, canal bridges, reflections, and the life that ebbs and flows with the lakes, I realized that I was capturing more than just photographs; I was documenting the spirit of a place, a shared experience of growing up, playing, working, and gathering around meals by the water's edge. Here, food is more than sustenance—it is the language of hospitality and belonging, a way of offering comfort that says, "You are home." My friend Yoshi, a chef and recipe contributor to this book, once told me that "sacrifices must be made for good food." For him, preparing a meal is not just about the flavors; it is an act of devotion, a way to be part of life's pivotal moments—first dates, weddings, anniversaries, and even funerals.

He finds meaning in the ability to nourish others, to serve a community in its most intimate moments, just as the lakes have witnessed those moments in the passing of time. He says that restaurant work, like life in Florida, "takes a village"—it's about pulling people together around a table, sharing a meal that becomes a small but vital thread in the fabric of the place.

This book is a blend of photography, prose, poetry, and recipes, each chosen to reflect the communal nature of growing up and living in Florida. The poems are moments of reflection, capturing the rhythm of life by the lakes, while the recipes are an invitation to gather—an echo of the many meals shared beside these waters, filled with flavors that speak of home and heritage. Together, they aim to preserve the feeling of the lakes—their quiet strength, their ability to hold stories, and their unchanging presence through the passing of time.

Yet, as I write this, Hurricane Milton churns into a Category 5 storm, reminding me that Florida's resilience runs as deep as its roots. Like the cypress trees that weather each storm and stand strong, the people of Florida have learned to endure—storm after storm, change after change. Hurricanes, politics, explosive population growth—each seems to chip away at the essence of Old Florida, but Florida is not that easily changed. The landscape holds its own, refusing to bend to the will of newcomers. Here, it is Florida that does the shaping—those who come here must learn to adapt, to understand the language of its seasons, its storms, its stillness, and its floods. Each passing storm, each summer heatwave, hardens us, leaving behind those who have learned what it means to survive.

Survival in Florida has never been a solitary endeavor. Just as the cypress roots intertwine beneath the surface, so do the lives of Floridians. It takes community and kindness to thrive in a landscape that demands resilience. You cannot face a 12-foot storm surge or the chaos of fallen trees and broken buildings alone. It's a neighborhood pulling together that overcomes the destruction. When the power goes out, it is often a neighbor you've never spoken to who shows up with a cup of coffee and a smile. And when floodwaters steal away everything you own, it is your community that will bend their backs beside you, helping to gut your home and rebuild.

In Florida, we learn that you don't truly own anything. Time, water, and nature will take it all away in an instant. Community, family, friends—people are really all you have. And in the face of each new storm, we find strength not just in ourselves, but in each other. That spirit, that connection, is what I hope to capture through Lake Front. This book is both a tribute to the unyielding strength of the cypress trees and the people who have grown with them, and an invitation to see the lakes through my eyes, to walk alongside me through past summers and future mornings, and to find themselves in the stories that ripple across the water.

Rooted Together. In Florida, possessions are temporary, but the strength of family and community is enduring. After Hurricane Milton, the true value isn't in what was lost to nature but in what was held on to—each aother. As this family clears away fallen debris, they remind us that in the face of time and nature's cycles, it's the connections we share that weather every storm.

SWAMP SIDE BISCUITS & GRAVY

Ingredients:

For the Biscuits:

- 2 cups all-purpose flour
- 1 1/2 tbsp baking powder
- 1 tbsp raw sugar
- 1/2 tbsp kosher salt
- 6 oz (3/4 stick) cold unsalted butter, cubed
- 3/4 cup buttermilk

For the Gravy:

- 1/2 lb ground pork
- 1/2 lb ground gator
- 2 tsp ground thyme
- 2 tsp ground sage
- 4 dashes cayenne pepper-based hot sauce (e.g., Tabasco, Cholula)
- 1/2 cup all-purpose flour
- 4 cups milk
- Kosher salt, to taste
- Coarse ground black pepper, to taste
- 4 oz bacon grease or 2 oz oil

Instructions:

For the Biscuits:

1: Combine flour, baking powder, raw sugar, and kosher salt in a mixing bowl. Add cold butter and mix until the butter pieces are pea sized. Gradually add buttermilk, mixing gently until a slightly crumbly dough forms.

2: Turn the dough onto a lightly floured surface. Pat into a rectangle and fold into thirds, like a letter. Turn and flatten into a rectangle, repeating the folding process two more times.
Preheat oven to 450°F (230°C). Line a baking pan with parchment paper or use a seasoned cast iron skillet.

3: Preheat oven to 450°F (230°C). Line a baking pan with parchment paper or use a seasoned cast iron skillet.
4: Cut the dough into circles using a pastry cutter, or scoop with a spoon and place on the baking sheet. Ensure biscuits are slightly touching.
5: Let the biscuits rest for 10 minutes.
6: Bake for 15-17 minutes, until the tops are golden brown.

For the Gravy:

1: Heat bacon grease or oil in a saucepan over medium heat. Add ground pork and ground gator, cooking until medium.
2: Stir in ground thyme, ground sage, and hot sauce. Continue cooking until the meat is fully cooked.
3: Add flour, stirring constantly until it turns a blonde color, forming a roux.
4: Gradually add milk, stirring until smooth. Simmer until desired thickness is reached. Season with salt and pepper

To Serve:

1: Place biscuits in a bowl and ladle gravy over the top. Enjoy!

Through the Oaks and Cypress. The sunset quietly descends over Lake Howard. In the quiet moments like this, the balance between time, nature, and resilience becomes clear. The lake and trees stand as they always have, witnesses to the cycles of nature, carrying the weight of the past while embracing the fleeting beauty of the present.

Growing Up on the Water

SUMMER ECHOES

We were bold then, daring the water to keep us,
Launching ourselves into the blue with sunburned arms,
Flipping and splashing until we blurred into summer.
Back then, days were endless like the lake's horizon—
We believed in the weight of the heat,
The way it held us down to earth, like hands on our shoulders.
Afternoons unfolded like picnic blankets,
Spread wide on lawns littered with pine needles,
And evenings smelled of charcoal and fresh-cut grass.
We ran barefoot over sun-warmed docks,
Our toes tracing lines into ancient wood.
Time held its breath as we made our leaps,
And the world paused in the ripples we left behind.
Now, those echoes find us still,
Returning in the sway of Spanish moss,
And in the hush of twilight, we hear them calling—
Ghost voices that linger, pressing through the past.

Chapter Page: Assorted Family Photos. This series of photos captures the essence of a childhood spent along the lakes, surrounded by family, friends, and the rhythm of nature. The images show a mix of fishing triumphs, playful moments, and timeless lessons, from dockside adventures to teaching the next generation how to steer the boat. Together, they reflect a way of life on the Chain of Lakes where traditions and outdoor skills are passed down, and where the bond between the lakes and the people growing up around them is as strong as the waters that tie them together.

Photo Page: Assorted Family Photos. In these cherished photos, the joy of childhood on the lakes comes alive with playful abandon, showing days spent under the Florida sun. From flips in the yard to first fishing trips and family moments captured at the docks, each snapshot is a nostalgic reminder of simpler times. It's about the little victories, the sunny afternoons, and the feeling that, growing up on the Chain of Lakes, there was no place you'd rather be.

My granddaddy's house sat proudly on the shore of Lake Conine, part of the North Chain—the Little Chain—within the larger Chain of Lakes that we called home. This house was more than just a place to sleep; it was a gathering spot, a family hub that thrived with the constant ebb and flow of relatives coming and going. My mother's siblings often came back home to visit, bringing along their children—my cousins—who felt every bit as close as brothers and sisters. For an only child like me, this house turned into a place where the mundane transformed into the extraordinary, where a typical day could be interrupted by a surprise visit and a new adventure.

The lake was our playground, its waters mirroring our boundless energy. We would ride our bikes straight off the boat dock into the lake, laughing as we splashed down. The canoe, forever bobbing at the water's edge, became our gateway to explore hidden nooks along the shore. Fishing rods, grass shrimp, and afternoons spent on the dock were the rhythms that marked our time. The lake seemed to know us, to hold the memory of our laughter as we ran barefoot, gathering around to dig out the sand spurs that had found their way into our feet. Bruises and scratches were part of the game, and we never let the grown-ups in on what we "got into." Some stories were meant to be kept between cousins, a secret world that the lake seemed to keep for us.

Yet, as personal as these memories feel, they are far from unique. Growing up on the Chain meant sharing a way of life that many others experienced. These waters held entire childhoods within their depths, offering the same freedom and discovery to anyone who ventured to their shores. It was here that neighborhood kids learned to swim, cast their first fishing lines, and discover the thrill of being pulled behind a boat, even if the speed scared us a little. The Chain was our backdrop, and it connected us all—our stories woven together like the interconnected lakes themselves. It was a place where every child knew the satisfaction of catching their first bass or felt the thrill of spotting an alligator sunning on the shore.

Restoring this world through the photographs my mother took was a deeply personal project. The images, spanning three decades from 1974 to 2004, capture moments of everyday life along the lakes—quiet scenes and chaotic ones, adventure and rest.Time has worn these photos;

some faces have faded, and the edges of memory have blurred. Yet, in digitally restoring them, we preserved something more than just the images. We preserved the feeling of those summer days, the sense of community that comes from shared sunburns, fish stories, and the unbroken bond between family and water. This collaboration between my mother and me became a way to hold on to a piece of our story and, in turn, the story of so many who found their childhood on these waters. Through the process of editing and revitalizing these images, I realized that I was not just documenting my past—I was preserving a piece of collective memory, a story shared by those whose lives the Chain has shaped.

And there were always family meals—moments that anchored us amidst all the chaos and fun. No matter how many cousins or neighbors showed up, there was always a card table and folding chairs pulled out from somewhere, ensuring that everyone had a seat at the table. It was as if the food magically multiplied, always enough to accommodate unexpected guests. Watching families on TV, it sometimes seemed like we grew up with less, but looking back now, I realize the abundance we had—family, food, time, each other, and the lakes themselves.

Our picnics weren't confined to the dock; they became part of the adventure. We'd pack up sandwiches, chips, and drinks in the boat and navigate the Chain to reach Lake Eloise. Pulling up to the tire floats, we'd settle in to watch the Cypress Gardens ski show, a front-row seat to the spectacle on the water. Afterward, we'd cruise over to the shade beneath a stand of cypress trees, where we'd swim and eat our lunch, letting the gentle sounds of the lake surround us. By the time we headed back, sunburnt and exhausted, we were filled with a simple happiness that seemed to come as naturally as the breeze over the water.

In a way, the lakes raised us all. We were molded by the same forces—summer storms that swept through, endless days spent on the water, and the communities that pulled together through every change and challenge. My mother's photographs, though intimate and tied to our family, hold a mirror to the shared spirit of those who know the Chain as intimately as I do. It's in the joy of a child catching their first fish, in the glow of a sunset reflected on the water, in the way neighbors became family when help was needed. These images, old and worn, speak to anyone who has ever been shaped by these lakes, anyone who has felt their heart tied to these waters.

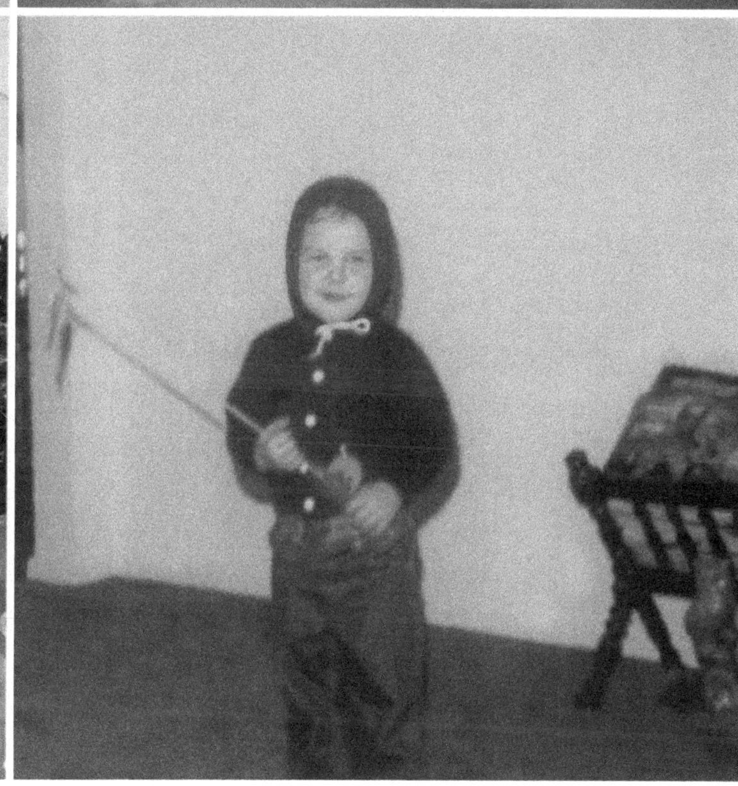

Assorted Family Photos. With each passing year, the Chain of Lakes becomes a constant backdrop for new adventures, from boxing matches on the patio to riding the wake for the first time. Family and wildlife share in the simple joys, as lessons learned in youth echo through time. This restoration project preserves the many layers of childhood exploration and lakeside wonder.

CHAIN OF LAKES CUBAN

Ingredients:

- 4 slices Cuban bread or crusty baguette
- 8 slices slow-roasted pork
- 8 slices thin-sliced smoked ham
- 4 slices Swiss cheese
- 4 tbsp key lime mustard spread (blend 2 tbsp mustard with 1 tbsp key lime juice and 1 tbsp honey)
- 8 bread-and-butter pickles

Instructions

1: Split the Cuban bread and spread key lime mustard on each side.
2: Layer smoked ham, roast pork, Swiss cheese, and bread-and butter pickles on the bread.
3: Press the sandwich gently to keep the layers together.
4: Chill in the refrigerator for 30 minutes to allow the flavors to meld.
5: Cut in half and serve cold, perfect for a picnic by the lake.

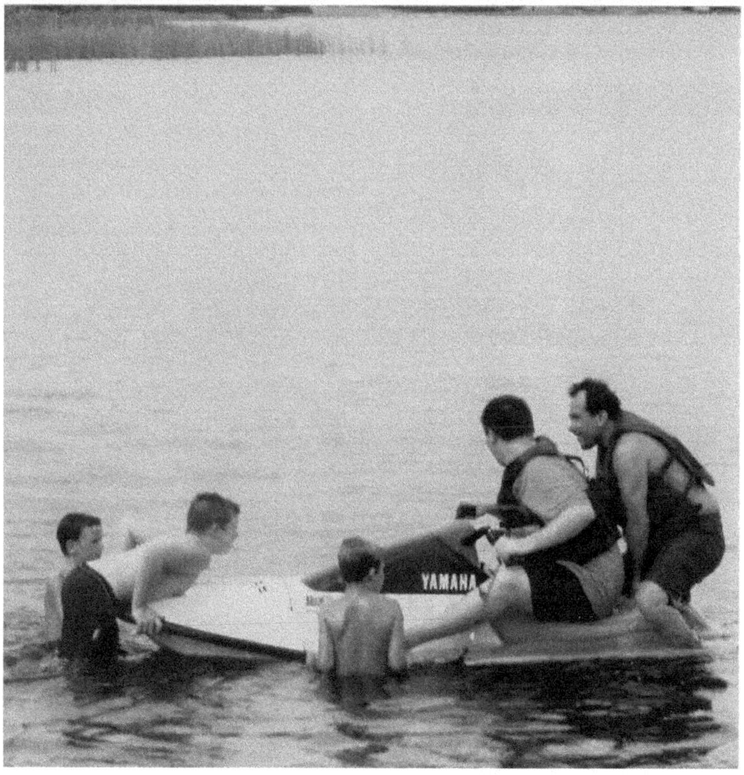

Assorted Family Photos. This collection of memories captures the unfiltered joy, adventures, and bonds of childhood on the Chain. Whether it's a proud moment showing off the day's catch, daring rescues with water sports equipment, or the creative mischief of being caged in homemade contraptions, these snapshots tell the tale of an upbringing filled with nature and family at the center. Each image reflects the freedom and spontaneity that defined our days on the water, always reminding us that the lake was as much a teacher as it was a playground.

Between Land and Water

RIPPLES OF JOY

Morning breaks with the hum of a motor's start,
Sending waves shivering through the lake's skin.
Sunlight scatters like glass shards on the surface,
And we carve circles through water's memory,
Each turn a bright cut that carries our laughter.
Our joy ripples out, rippling back,
Tangled in the reeds, caught in the roots.
Herons glide low, shadows grazing water,
And the lake remembers what we've forgotten—
The days we cast, the lines we lost,
Fish flipping silver into the sun's warm hands.
We dance with the wind, the warmth, the open sky,
Not knowing the day is slipping away,
Until the sun dips westward,
Leaning into the night's embrace,
And we leave our trails behind—
Small wakes, unbroken,
Echoes that whisper long after we've gone.

Chapter Page: Rails and Ripples. Perched above the gentle flow of the canal, the boy waits—fishing line in hand, feet dangling just above the water. The quiet hum of passing trains above is a reminder of the world's constant motion, but here, in this stillness, he's found a moment of peace. The tracks may lead elsewhere, but today, his focus is on the ripples below.

Photo Page: Memories Made. Floating on the lake, with rods in hand and no rush to be anywhere, it's a scene of pure Florida life — where time stands still, and the only sharks you'll see are the playful ones painted on the side of the boat—at least in the Chain.

Suncruiser
SHARK
PATROL
FL 8205MN

Summers on the Chain of Lakes were a blur of motion—days marked by the whirr of boat engines, the gentle lap of water against aluminum hulls, and the unmistakable hum of excitement in the air. For generations, Winter Haven has been synonymous with water skiing, a place where the sport wasn't just an activity but a way of life. It was here that Cypress Gardens—once dubbed the "Water Ski Capital of the World"—made its mark, drawing in visitors from all over to witness daring tricks and graceful ballet lines skimming across the water.

But for us, skiing wasn't about the spectacle; it was about the everyday thrill of rising up on a pair of skis behind the boat, feeling the lake beneath our feet, and the pull of the rope as it lifted us out of the water. My family lived for those moments, the way the water carved around their skis, each turn a brushstroke against the glassy lake. I always admired their effortless grace, even though I could never quite master it myself. While they glided between the buoys, their forms sleek against the sky, I watched from the boat, cheering them on and finding my own peace in the gentle bobbing of the waves.

Winter Haven's history is deeply tied to the Chain of Lakes and the water-skiing legacy it fostered. It wasn't just about Cypress Gardens, with its elaborate shows and acrobatics; it was about the countless families who took to the water, eager to learn and make their own mark. Weekends saw clusters of boats gathered near the best slalom spots, where beginners took their first unsteady rides while seasoned skiers zigzagged through obstacle courses with ease. From Lake Eloise to the quieter stretches of the North Chain, the lakes held the stories of those who skied before us—stories that were as much about perseverance as they were about fun. It was a kind of dance, a way to feel both free and rooted in the same breath, suspended between the rush of the water and the steady pull of home.

On the Southern Chain, Lake Winterset emerged as a natural gathering place, adding a different rhythm to the life of the lakes. Known for its social scene, Lake Winterset became the backdrop for spontaneous flotillas—boaters tying up together, creating a floating neighborhood where laughter and music drifted over the water. It was a place where the everyday and the extraordinary blurred together, where locals and newcomers alike found a sense of community under the Florida sun.

These gatherings became their own kind of tradition, a testament to the way Floridians adapt to the lakes' way of life, turning weekends into celebrations and quiet afternoons into shared memories.

The camaraderie on the lakes wasn't limited to organized events—it was woven into every encounter. If a boat broke down on the water, help was never far away. A wave from the bow or a simple shout would bring another boater alongside, offering a tow back to the nearest dock or lending a spare part to get the engine running again. It didn't matter if you were lifelong friends or strangers; on the Chain of Lakes, you were bound by a shared love for the water. Advice flowed as freely as the waves—where the bass were biting that morning, the best spot to drop a line under the shade of an overhanging oak, or the smoothest stretch for a late afternoon slalom run.

This sense of community extended beyond the water. At the marinas where boats fueled up and stories were exchanged, families from all over Winter Haven gathered to share tips, catch up, and swap fish tales. It was common to see kids from different families learning to ski together, taking turns behind the boat as their parents shared coolers and conversations on the shore. The lakes became a place where lives intertwined as naturally as the cypress roots, building friendships that lasted long after the sun set behind the tree line.

Even if I never joined in those dances, I understood their rhythm. Watching my brothers and cousins slice through the water, I saw more than just their skill; I saw a continuation of a tradition that belonged to our town, one that shaped our summers and stitched us together. The lakes, with their sprawling waterways and hidden coves, provided a stage for our small triumphs, a place where we could all be a part of something bigger. In the end, it didn't matter if you were on the skis or in the boat, on the shore or under the sun—what mattered was the connection we shared, the way the lakes carried our stories, old and new, in each ripple that reached the shore.

Lake Winterset's spirit—its parties, its spontaneous gatherings, and its sense of community—echoed the values that have always made life on the Chain of Lakes so special. It became a modern version of those early days when Cypress Gardens dazzled with water ballets, yet it kept alive the essence of what it means to live here: connection, shared joy, and a deep-rooted love for the water that defines us.

Set Up on Winterset. Families settle into the calm waters of Lake Winterset, with boats anchored and umbrellas raised. It's a scene of laid-back Florida living, where the lake becomes an extension of home—a perfect spot for sharing stories, laughter, and a day in the sun.

LAKE BREEZE MUSCADINE SUN TEA

Ingredients:

- 8 cups cold water
- 6 black tea bags
- 1 cup muscadine grapes, halved and smashed
- Ice and sliced lemon, for serving

Instructions

1: In a large glass jar, add black tea bags and smashed muscadine grapes. Fill with water.
2: Cover and place the jar in direct sunlight for 3-4 hours.
3: Remove the tea bags and strain out the smashed grapes. Chill the tea for 1-2 hours.
4: Serve over ice with a slice of lemon.

Down on the Dock. Under the warm Florida sun, a kid finds peace at the water's edge, embracing the simple pleasures of lake life. While the adults are busy in the boathouse, he's content, enjoying the tranquility that the lakeside offers, a reminder of childhood's unhurried pace.

Reflections of Home

HARBORING PEACE

Windows reflect the restless shimmer of waves,
As houses hold their breath along the shore.
Wooden porches cradle the weight of afternoons,
Sipping time like iced tea, one quiet hour at a time.
Cypress roots curl into the earth below,
Tethering dreams to the sand and waterline.
It is here that morning fog curls into the trees,
Whispering secrets of the lake's stillness—
A heron's call, a distant engine's murmur.
And on quiet evenings, orange blossoms drift in,
Tangling with laughter that spills from open windows.
We find our peace in this gentle holding,
In the way the sun sinks low, spilling gold over the water,
And every dusk is an unspoken promise—
That this place, this quiet, will wait for us,

Harboring the weight of our return.

Chapter Page: The Lake House. Framed by ancient cypress trees, the boathouse rests on the water's edge, its reflection rippling in the calm lake. A place where boats find shelter and the rhythm of the water meets the steady hum of life by the shore.

Photo Page: The Waiting Chair. An empty chair, patiently watching over the water's edge, invites quiet reflection. Here, time slows, and the world becomes a little simpler—just you, the trees, and the soft ripple of the lake.

Life along the lakes of Winter Haven unfolds like a slow-moving current, steady and timeless. The homes that dot the shoreline are more than just buildings—they are vessels of history, containing the echoes of generations that have shaped this town. The shores of Lake Howard and Lake Cannon have witnessed the rhythms of life: quiet mornings under the shade of ancient cypress trees, and afternoons filled with the hum of conversation drifting from boat docks. These are homes built on stories, where each wave carries whispers of the past.

Winter Haven's roots reach deep into Florida's history, beginning with the earliest inhabitants, the Timucua and Calusa peoples, whose lives intertwined with these waters long before European settlers arrived. As the Seminole people later moved into the area, led by figures like Chief Chipco during the Seminole Wars, they too became part of this land's story, their presence felt in the rich natural landscape that has remained. In the early 20th century, when the area began to attract American settlers after the United States acquired Florida, families came seeking a new start, drawn by the promise of fertile land and the allure of the lakes. The first settlers established small communities, carving out a life on the edge of these waters. As railroads expanded through Florida, the region blossomed, and Winter Haven was officially incorporated in 1911.

The lakes, with their glassy surfaces and hidden coves, became both a playground and a sanctuary for these families. For generations, these waters have been a place where time slows, where family gatherings unfold on wooden docks and in screened porches overlooking the rippling shoreline. From picnics shaded by live oaks to lazy afternoons in a well-loved Adirondack chair, the lakeside has always offered space for reflection and connection.

One of the most enduring stories is that of 1806 N. Lake Howard Drive, a home built in 1938 and later purchased by Dick and Julie Pope, the founders of Cypress Gardens. It was here that the property became a symbol of local history, a landmark for the town. The myth that Burt Reynolds once owned the home has persisted through the years, a story that many wanted to believe. But despite the allure, Polk County records reveal that the home passed instead from the Popes to the Mathley family, and later to Andy Thornal, a name familiar to many for his connection to outdoor adventures.

Yet, it's not just the unraveling of a local mystery that makes this place significant. A storied footbridge connects the Pope home to the property across the canal, where Dick Pope's brother Malcolm lived. This small bridge, now a part of local lore, became a symbol of connection over water—a quiet reminder of the ties that bind families and homes in Winter Haven.

Life on the water often spills over into a sense of community that transcends property lines. Neighbors become friends over shared cups of coffee on dockside patios, exchanging stories of the day's catch or the best spots to watch the sunset. On weekends, boats are often seen clustered together, with families trading fishing tips, towing kids on inflatable tubes, or offering a hand when a motor falters. It's a place where strangers are quick to become friends, bonded by a shared love for the lakes and the lifestyle they offer.

The houses themselves, from modest cottages to sprawling lakefront estates, tell stories of their own. Many have stood for generations, their walls absorbing the laughter and secrets of the families that have lived within them. Some were built by the first waves of settlers, while others are newer, yet all share a connection to the lakes that remain the town's lifeblood. They face the water with wide windows and open porches, capturing every breeze and reflecting the golden glow of the setting sun. In these spaces, history lingers—whether it's in the weathered wood of a dock that's seen countless summer afternoons or in the overgrown gardens where children once played hide and seek. And as much as the past is present in these places, so too is the promise of new stories being made, as younger generations discover their own love for the lake life, carrying forward a tradition that feels as enduring as the cypress trees that line the shores.

Cannon-Howard Arch. The Spanish moss drapes like lace from the ancient oak, creating a natural archway over the quiet canal—another reminder that here, nature shapes the path forward, always offering shelter and mystery.

DORIS' MACARONI SALAD

Ingredients:

- 1 box (16 oz) elbow macaroni
- 1 green bell pepper, diced
- 2 tomatoes, diced
- 1 1/2 cups mayonnaise (more as needed)
- Salt, to taste
- 1 tbsp olive oil

Instructions

1: In a large pot, bring water to a boil with salt and olive oil.
2: Add elbow macaroni and cook for 10 minutes, or until tender. Drain and transfer to a cold bowl.
3: Stir in 1/2 cup mayonnaise while the macaroni is still warm. Place in the refrigerator to cool.
4: Once the macaroni has cooled, add the diced bell pepper and tomatoes, then stir in another 1 cup mayonnaise.
5: Before serving, check the salad for consistency and seasoning. Add additional mayonnaise and salt if needed.
6: Serve chilled.

Lookin' Out My Back Door. Through the curtain of Spanish moss, the view from the porch is a quiet sanctuary. A backyard framed by cypress giants, where the lake becomes an ever-present reminder of the life that flows just beyond the trees.

Wild Hearts

THE QUIET ONES

They dwell at the water's edge, in the reeds,
Where shadows slip between ripples, unseen.
The anhinga spreads its wings to dry in the sun,
A silhouette that speaks to ancient skies.
Turtles haul their heavy shells onto logs,
Silent as the cypress knees that cradle them.
Alligators drift beneath the glassy surface,
Eyes just breaking the water's skin—
Cold-blooded guardians, older than our stories.
We are visitors in their kingdom,
Wading through the whispers of their world,
Wondering at the rhythm they know—
The way the sun moves, the language of rain.
In their stillness, they hold what we've lost:
The quiet between heartbeats,
The pull of moonlit tides, the hum of hidden things.
They leave us only traces, a shadow slipping into dusk,
And the lake holds them close,
As it once held us all.

Chapter Page: Born on the Bayou. With the fading light of dusk reflecting off the water, a quiet moment of triumph unfolds. In a place where the wild and the domestic meet, this is the Florida we know—where every day brings a new story to the water's edge.

Photo Page: Nesting. Tucked away in the thick of the branches, the Great Blue Heron finds sanctuary. Here, in the quiet embrace of nature, life continues—hidden, steady, and undisturbed.

The Chain of Lakes in Winter Haven is more than a collection of scenic waters—it's a living ecosystem, a habitat that supports a vibrant community of plants and animals. The lakes, from Lake Cannon to Lake Howard, are home to an array of species, each contributing to the delicate balance of this natural environment. The steady call of herons, the sight of an otter slipping into the water, or the flash of a largemouth bass beneath the surface are daily reminders of the lakes' dynamic life.

The natural beauty of these lakes isn't just a backdrop for human activities; it's a crucial part of Winter Haven's identity. Recognizing the need to protect this resource, local initiatives have grown around conservation and restoration. Programs emphasize sustainable water management and the health of the lakes. Comprehensive plans focus on viewing water as a precious resource, aiming to improve water quality, enhance stormwater capture, and recharge aquifers—efforts that help maintain the integrity of the lakes that define the city's landscape.

Winter Haven's lakes are at the head of the Peace River watershed, which means that the health of these waters has downstream effects, extending all the way to Charlotte Harbor. This makes conservation efforts even more significant. Organizations and community volunteers often engage in projects to restore shorelines, reduce nutrient pollution, and control invasive plant species that threaten the native flora and fauna. These efforts help to maintain the water clarity and quality, supporting the myriad of species that depend on these waters for survival.

However, as Winter Haven grows, so does the challenge of balancing development with conservation. Overdevelopment, both residential and commercial, poses significant threats to the delicate ecosystem of the Chain of Lakes. New housing developments and commercial spaces increase pressure on the natural landscape, often leading to the loss of wetlands that act as natural buffers. These wetlands filter stormwater and trap pollutants before they reach the lakes, contributing to cleaner water and a more balanced ecosystem. Without these natural barriers, increased runoff from paved surfaces introduces pollutants like fertilizers, pesticides, and other chemicals directly into the water. This runoff can cause nutrient loading, leading to harmful algal blooms that deplete oxygen levels, harm fish populations, and disrupt the entire ecological balance of the lakes.

The wildlife of Winter Haven's lakes is a study in adaptation. Alligators slide beneath the surface, while ospreys hover above, diving to snatch fish in their talons. The shallows are thick with cattails and pickerelweed, where turtles bask, and frogs sing through the night. Even the smallest inhabitants, like the snails that clean the lakebed, play a role in the broader ecosystem, creating a web of life that is as interconnected as the lakes themselves.

The ongoing development also contributes to shoreline erosion, which further degrades water quality and threatens habitats. The stability of the shorelines is essential for maintaining the clarity of the lakes and supporting the many species that rely on them—from fish and turtles to birds like herons and ospreys. Local conservation efforts emphasize the need for sustainable development practices and preserving wetland areas. Initiatives like wetland treatment parks help mitigate some of the negative impacts by using natural processes to filter stormwater before it reaches the lakes.

The community's relationship with the lakes is one of both enjoyment and stewardship. Conservation groups and residents often collaborate, organizing clean-up events, shoreline plantings, and educational programs to foster a sense of responsibility toward these waters. The goal is to ensure that the beauty and biodiversity of the lakes endure for generations to come, maintaining the balance that allows life to thrive in and around the waters.

In the end, the health of the lakes directly impacts the quality of life for those who call Winter Haven home. The lakes, with their rich biodiversity and delicate ecosystems, serve as a reminder that nature and community are intertwined, and that the future of Winter Haven depends on how well these waters are cared for. Amid the push for progress, there is a growing recognition that sustainable practices must be prioritized to safeguard this vital resource. The lakes stand as a testament to the region's natural wealth and as a call to action to protect what makes Winter Haven special.

I Like You. There's a quiet understanding in the way this gentle giant looks back at you—trusting, curious, and calm. In this moment, you realize: the connection between us and nature is as simple and as powerful as a shared gaze.

BAYOU BLACKENED GATOR

Ingredients:

- 1 lb gator filets or tenders (cut filets into strips)
- 1 cup kosher salt
- 1/2 cup oil
- 1 cup Tony Chachere's Creole seasoning
- 2 tbsp smoked paprika
- 2 tbsp granulated garlic
- tbsp dried thyme leaves
- 2 tbsp butter

Instructions

1: In a bowl, cover the gator meat with cold water and 1 cup kosher salt, ensuring the water is 1 inch above the meat. Soak overnight.
2: Drain, rinse, and pat the gator meat dry in the morning.
3: Mix oil, Tony Chachere's Creole seasoning, smoked paprika, granulated garlic, and dried thyme in a separate bowl.
4: Add the gator to the seasoning mixture and let marinate for 4-6 hours.
5: Heat a cast iron skillet over medium heat. Once hot, melt butter in the skillet.
6: Add a few pieces of marinated gator to the hot skillet, cooking 3-6 pieces at a time to avoid overcrowding.
7: Cook for 3-5 minutes per side or until the sides turn white and the internal temperature reaches 148°F (64°C).
8: Serve hot.

Serpent of Enlightenment. Coiled in stillness atop the temple roof, the serpent symbolizes both rebirth and spiritual awakening. In the quiet of the water's reflection, it serves as a reminder of the path toward enlightenment—a journey inward, where wisdom is earned through patience and the harmony of all living things.

Rooted in Time

SILENT GUARDIANS

They stand, limbs tangled with clouds,
Casting shadows that stretch across decades.
Their bark is a rough memory, each groove a line,
Marking years like rings beneath the surface.
Beneath the waterline, their roots weave deep,
Touching the secrets buried in silt and time.
They weather wildness—
Hurricanes bending their backs but never breaking them.
They bear the edge of each storm,
Draw strength from the earth's dark bones.
They reach for stars spun out and lost,
Beyond the edges of memory, beyond even us.
In winter, they wear the sky like an old coat,
In summer, they cradle the light.
And still they stand, as we drift past,
Watching the rise and fall of our days.
The cypress remain, steadfast and still,
Their stories written in water, told in silence,
Turning each new breeze into a verse.

Chapter Page: Time Worn. The cypress stands alone, weathered by decades of wind and water. Its branches, some outstretched, some broken, tell a quiet story of endurance. Time, like the water beneath it, moves steadily onward, but this tree remains—a testament to the strength found in resilience.

Photo Page: Then God Smiled. The sky opened above the cypress, casting light and shadow in a perfect balance. The trees, rooted deep in the water, stood in still reverence—timeless witnesses to creation.

Cypress trees are more than just towering sentinels along the shores of Winter Haven's lakes; they are, in many ways, guardians of the spirit of this place. Their roots extend deep into the muck and murk of the lakebed, anchoring not only themselves but the memories, stories, and very essence of life that clings to these waters. These trees, ancient and steadfast, hold a reverence that feels almost sacred—a connection to something beyond time, as enduring as the gentle laps of water against the shore.

When you stand under the canopy of a cypress tree, with its branches draped in Spanish moss like nature's own stained glass, it's easy to feel that these trees know something we do not. They whisper of times before roads and houses, of when the Timucua and Calusa tribes walked these lands, crafting canoes from their trunks, gliding through waters as timeless as the trees themselves. To them, the cypress was a vessel—both literally and metaphorically—a means to traverse the waters, but also a bridge between the seen and the unseen. Even as they carved the wood, they left its spirit intact, carrying with them the essence of the tree into their journeys.

The Seminoles, who came later, found a kinship with the cypress as well, understanding its resilience. These trees, like the people who came to live among them, could bend without breaking, their roots reaching out into the waters, their trunks standing firm against the fiercest winds. It's no wonder that cypress groves were seen as places of refuge and reflection—a sanctuary amid the chaos, a space where the veil between the material and spiritual world seemed thinner. The cypress, after all, knows how to endure. It stands through the battering rains and howling winds of Florida's hurricanes, swaying but rarely falling, offering its lesson in resilience to those who seek it.

For those who live on these lakes today, the cypress tree remains a symbol of permanence in a world that seems to change too quickly. Its presence speaks to the eternal cycle of life and death, of renewal and decay. Even when a cypress falls, its wood, resistant to rot, remains in the water, becoming a new habitat—a home for fish, a perch for turtles, a nursery for countless creatures. The cypress does not mourn its passing but instead transforms, offering itself back to the waters that sustained it, its essence lingering in the lakes' shadows long after it's gone.

The ancient Egyptians believed the cypress was a tree of life and death, linking it to the afterlife, while in the Christian tradition, the cypress has been seen as a symbol of immortality and being of God's beloved people, its evergreen nature a reminder of life beyond the grave. In mythology, it is often the guardian of the threshold, standing at the border between the living and the dead, a tree that bridges worlds. And here, on the shores of Winter Haven, the cypress continues in this role—not just as a symbol, but as a living testament to the endurance of nature, the persistence of memory, and the interconnectedness of all things.

It's no coincidence that the cypress thrives where water meets land, in the liminal space where one world blurs into another. It is a tree that holds the edges together, reminding us that life is not just in the grand gestures but in the quiet persistence, the way roots seek water, the way leaves find the sun. The cypress knows that survival is an act of balance—a lesson that these lakes teach as well. They are a home to all who seek refuge in their shade, to the herons that roost in their branches, to the fish that shelter beneath their knees, to the children who grow up playing in their shadows. Each life, large and small, finds its place in the circle that the cypress holds.

As development presses in from all sides, it is easy to forget what the cypress knows—that these lakes, this land, are not just resources to be used but sacred spaces to be revered. The cypress reminds us of our role as stewards, of the duty to protect what endures. To lose a cypress is not just to lose a tree; it is to lose a piece of the soul of these lakes, a thread in the intricate web that binds water, land, and life together. In its quiet, unwavering way, the cypress invites us to remember—to listen to the stories that the wind carries through its branches, to the secrets whispered among its roots, and to honor the connections that hold us all, like roots in the water, steady against the currents of time.

And the Light Broke. Through the branches, the light poured down, illuminating the Spanish moss in soft brilliance. The cypress stood tall, as if soaking in the radiance of a new beginning.

SWAMP CAPRESE SALAD

Ingredients:

For the Citrus Vinaigrette:

- 4 oz orange juice (preferably with pulp)
- 2 oz white balsamic vinegar
- 2 oz honey
- 2 tbsp dijon mustard
- Juice of 1 lemon
- 4 oz vegetable oil (substitute any oil except olive oil)
- 1 oz fresh parsley
- 1/2 tbsp kosher salt
- 1 tsp black pepper

For the Salad:

- 1 jar/can of palm hearts (swamp cabbage)
- 1 lb muscadine grapes (use a mix of colors, if desired)
- 1 lb sharp white cheddar cheese curds
- 3 fire roasted red bell peppers

Instructions:

For the Citrus Vinaigrette:

1: Combine orange juice, vinegar, salt, pepper, lemon juice, parsley,mustard and honey in a blender. Blend on high until fully mixed.
2: Reduce blender speed to medium and slowly pour in vegetable oil. Blend for an additional 30 seconds after the oil is incorporated.
3: Let sit while assembling the salad.

or the Salad:

1: Drain palm hearts, cut into bite-sized pieces, and place in a mixing bowl.
2: Cut muscadine grapes in half and add to the bowl.
3: Cut fire roasted red bell peppers into bite-sized pieces and add to the bowl.
4: Add cheese curds to the bowl.
5: Pour the citrus vinaigrette over the ingredients and gently stir until

And He Said, "That's Good." In the calm that followed, the trees and sky met in quiet harmony. The water mirrored the heavens, and the world, for just a moment, was whole.

Shadows of the Night

AFTER DARK

The night rises slow, like mist off the water,
Where neon bleeds across the surface,
And the bassline hums low through the open doors.
Laughter skips like pebbles over waves,
Mixing with the clinking of ice in glasses,
And the sizzle of fish pulled fresh from the fryer.
The lake holds the reflection of every light,
Turning each ripple into a pulse,
A heartbeat that follows us down the boardwalk.
Under the black canopy, we sway like palms,
Moving to rhythms that drift in the warm air,
With lanterns casting shadows that twist and stretch.
Out past the docks, night birds skim the water,
And somewhere a guitar bends into the dark,
Filling the spaces where words falter.
Here, where the city gives way to silence,
And the water listens, listens,
We find ourselves at the edge of what is,
And what might be, waiting just beyond the dark.

Chapter Page: Jessie's Neon Guitar. The glow of Jessie's iconic neon sign cuts through the night, casting a bright hum over the heart of Winter Haven. Beneath it, music pulses through the doors, inviting all who pass by to step inside and join the rhythm of the night.

Photo Page: After the Storm. The music returns to the waterfront as Saturday night unfolds at the Twisted Prop. Under the glow of string lights and the hum of conversation, the night feels alive again—resilient and unbroken, even after the storm has passed.

Winter Haven's social scene is as much a part of the lakes as the water itself. When the sun dips below the cypress-lined horizon and the skies begin to darken, the lakes reflect not just the moonlight, but the spirit of a town that knows how to come alive after dark. Here, evenings are for gathering—around tables, on barstools, or on a dock under the stars. The rhythm of Winter Haven pulses through these moments, each space offering a different beat, a different story, a different place where the community comes together.

On the lakefront, Old Man Franks stands as a relic of a simpler time, its weathered docks and mismatched furniture welcoming those who crave an easygoing atmosphere. The sound of laughter mixes with the splash of water against the pilings, patrons come in search of a cold beer and a warm story. Across the way, Harborside offers a different kind of lakefront experience—white tablecloths and waterfront views, boats tie up to their dock and wait for the next table while diners enjoy seafood and steak. It's a place for celebrations, where the sparkle of lights on the water makes every evening feel like a special occasion.

Further down the shoreline, Tanners Lakeside serves as a bridge between the laid-back and the lively. With its sprawling outdoor space and lineup of local bands, it's the kind of place where families gather for dinner while groups of friends sip cocktails on the patio. On breezy weekend nights, the air is filled with the sounds of guitar strings and the clinking of glasses, as regulars swap stories about the catch of the day and watch a sunset over the Chain.

The Twisted Prop and Caribbean Bay keep things a little more offbeat, drawing those who crave a touch of adventure with their nightlife. At the Prop, it's all about friends, family, and watching the sunset with a live band and great gator tail. And at Caribbean Bay, the vibe is relaxed but rhythmic, a place where karaoke and classic rock mixes with the hum of conversation, and a seat by the water can make you forget about the rest of the world, if only for a while. Both places remind you that a night out doesn't have to be polished—it just has to feel like home.

Downtown Winter Haven, though a bit farther from the lakes, captures the same spirit in its own way. Jessie's Lounge, tucked into a building on 3rd Street, has become a cornerstone of the live music scene. Inside, beneath the glow of old string lights and exposed brick, strangers become friends as they sway to the rhythm of blues and rock. Just next door, Jensen's Corner Bar offers a great social scene, where the hum of conversation mingles with the clinking of glasses, and patrons linger over carefully selected craft beers and local wines. It's the kind of place where you come for a drink and stay for a story, where every visit feels like a reunion.

For those looking for something a little more refined, The Ave Bar, nestled in the heart of downtown, offers a chic cocktail experience. Just steps from the Ritz Theatre and connected to the renowned Arabella's Ristorante, Ave Bar is where you gather before a night of fine dining or after a performance. Its sophisticated and warm here, the perfect balance between the lively energy of the town and quiet luxury. It's a place where you can escape for a while, enjoy a martini, and feel like you're part of the pulse of Winter Haven, even if you're away from the water for the evening There's a thread that ties these places together—an understanding that socializing in Winter Haven is more than just passing the time. It's about being known and knowing others, about finding connection in a shared love for the lakes, the music, the places that have shaped the town. At Gram Parsons Derry Down, that thread reaches deep into the town's musical roots. It's where history and melody merge, where the echoes of a young Gram Parsons and the spirit of country rock still linger in the old wood rafters. Today, it's a place where local musicians keep the tradition alive, their songs weaving new chapters into the town's story.

Then there's the easygoing, backyard rhythm of Grove Roots Brewery, where families and friends gather while kids chase each other through the open space, and dogs happily underfoot. It's a place where a Saturday afternoon with a pint in hand can stretch into an evening of live music, with the comforting feel of a neighborhood BBQ. There's a simplicity in the gatherings here—a game of cornhole, the chatter of old friends, and the warm hum of community that lingers long after the sun has dipped below the tree line.

The Social offers a different kind of gathering—a step into a hidden world where time seems to slow down. Behind its discreet entrance, the speakeasy vibe takes over, blending the allure of a 1920s jazz club with a modern flair. Here, specialty cocktails are crafted with care, served in a low-lit room where leather armchairs invite intimate conversations. It's a place where the energy is quieter, more contemplative, where you can savor each sip and each word, tucked away from the bustle outside, before stepping back into the night.

In each of these places, there's a sense that time moves differently here. It's a time measured not by the ticking of the clock, but by the rhythm of live music, the clink of a glass, the murmur of a conversation that carries on long after the last notes have faded. It's a rhythm that keeps the heart of Winter Haven beating, even as the shadows stretch long across the lakes and the night settles in. In these moments, whether on a dock or at a barstool, surrounded by the sounds of the lake or the strum of a guitar, you find yourself part of something bigger—a community that feels like it's always been here, where the night is as much about the place as it is about the people who fill it.

Jammin'. In this open space, the guitar mural watches over a place where music is more than just sound—it's the heartbeat of the night. Here, under the strings of art and sky, the notes play on, and the crowd moves with the rhythm, connected by the shared energy of the moment.

HURRICANE MILTON

Ingredients:

- 2 oz kumquat puree (blend fresh kumquats with a little water)
- 2 oz dark rum
- 1 oz light rum
- 2 oz passionfruit juice
- 1 oz tangerine juice
- 1 oz key lime juice
- 1 tbsp simple syrup
- Ice and kumquat slices, for garnish

Instructions

1: In a cocktail shaker, combine kumquat puree, dark rum, light rum, passionfruit juice, tangerine juice, key lime juice, and simple syrup with ice.
2: Shake well until thoroughly mixed and chilled.
3: Strain into a glass filled with ice.
4: Garnish with kumquat slices and serve immediately.

Full Throttle at Old Man Frank's. Under the soft glow of string lights, Old Man Frank's hums with life as the night deepens. Perched on the edge of the lake, it's a place where locals gather, the music mingling with the sound of the water, and the easygoing rhythm of the night takes over.

Unwritten Stories

HIDDEN WORDS

Where the bridges arch their backs over the canal,
Beneath the rumble of trains and the hum of tires,
Graffiti blooms in secret places—
Colors too bright for daylight, defiant and raw.
Names carved into the concrete ribs,
Bold confessions written in a rush of spray paint.
Here, the water carries messages,
Echoes of hands that touched the bridge's belly,
Marking time in a language only night understands.
The canal carries it all away—
Our questions, our hopes, the names we dared to write.
Rust clings to the steel beams overhead,
And each passing boat tells a story in its wake,
Leaving ripples to lap against painted stone.
We pass through this gallery of hidden voices,
Reading the layers of color and dust,
And the water, always moving, always flowing,
Knows the truth of every unsaid word.

Chapter Page: Flamingo Love Bridge. On this quiet canal bridge, a flamingo takes form, painted in bold strokes amidst symbols of love. It's a moment of expression left behind, speaking to those who pass beneath, capturing the essence of a city's hidden creativity and fleeting connection.

Photo Page: Blaze on the Bridge. This unassuming bridge carries more than just traffic over the water—it carries the names and symbols of those who've left their mark. Blaze, scrawled boldly beneath the concrete, captures a fleeting moment of expression, framed by the peaceful lake that stretches beyond.

Where the bridges stretch their backs across the canals, art blooms in secret places. Beneath the concrete arches and along the water's edge, graffiti-style murals whisper stories in colors too bright for daylight, their lines mingling with shadows and the hum of passing boats. These hidden galleries, known to few, are woven into the fabric of Winter Haven's waterways. They form a tapestry of images—flamingos, abstract forms, and bold letters—each adding a piece to the story of this place, one that speaks in the language of spray paint and whispered messages.

The canals, with their quiet flow, have long been a canvas for spontaneous creativity. Here, beneath the graffiti's layered paint, is a reminder of what it means to leave a mark, to share a message that echoes beneath the bridges long after the artist has gone. It's a place where art belongs to the water as much as it does to the walls, blending into the ripples and the reflections of palms above. These pieces, raw and unpolished, carry the pulse of a city that thrives on its connection to the lakes.

Yet, this spirit of expression doesn't stop at the canals. In downtown Winter Haven, murals from both local and international artists grace brick walls and building sides, turning the town into an open-air gallery. Works by artists like Gillian Fazio, whose mural titled "Haven" sings a tribute to the town's spirit, sit alongside the dynamic pieces by renowned Spanish artists David de la Mano and Pablo S. Herrero. Their murals, such as "The Calm" and "Cycle," weave images of nature and human figures, mirroring the balance that Winter Haven strikes between its lakes and urban life.

These downtown murals have transformed the cityscape, drawing visitors to explore alleyways and hidden corners in search of vibrant art. But even as these pieces gain recognition, the graffiti on the canal bridges remains an underground conversation—an echo of a different kind of artistry, one that is unsanctioned but no less vital. It hints at the potential for something more, a possibility that the bridges themselves could become part of a larger vision for public art in Winter Haven.

Imagine, if you will, these quiet canals transformed into a festival of murals—each bridge a new canvas, each concrete span a place for artists to tell their stories. Just as the waters of the Chain of Lakes connect neighborhoods and lives, so too could a series of murals connect the artistic spirit of this community. Such an event would bring together the raw energy of the graffiti artist with the careful craft of the muralist, turning the waterways into a new kind of gallery, where art and nature flow together.

This vision, though still unwritten, would be more than just a festival. It would be a way for Winter Haven to celebrate its identity, honoring both the hidden voices of the canals and the vibrant murals that now grace its downtown. It would invite visitors to navigate these waters not just to explore the beauty of the lakes but to see the stories unfolding on the walls above. Here, where water meets art, Winter Haven's bridges could become symbols of creativity—crossing the divide between tradition and innovation, between the quiet whispers of hidden art and the bold declarations of a new era.

In these imagined murals, we might see reflections of Winter Haven's past, of the cypress trees that bend with the wind, of the fish that swim in the shadows below. We might see nods to the graffiti that came before, preserved within new layers of color and line. And just as the lakes have held the stories of generations, these bridges, adorned with art, would hold a story of their own—a story of a town that understands the power of both the seen and the unseen, of what is shared and what is kept close, like secrets hidden beneath the surface of the water.

Gator's Gaze. Emerging from the side of the building, the larger-than-life gator watches over the city. Its fierce grin and sharp teeth remind passersby that in this place, wildness is never too far away—always part of the landscape, blending the natural world with urban art.

TOM'S TATERS

Ingredients:

- 4 large russet potatoes
- 4 tbsp salted butter
- 1 tsp smoked salt
- 1 tsp fresh rosemary, chopped
- 1 cup Monterey jack cheese, shredded

Instructions

1: Preheat the oven to 425°F (220°C).
2: Slice potatoes into discs of about 1 inch thick.
3: Score the top of each disk about 1/2 way through.
4: Coat pan with warm butter to prevent sticking.
5: Place potato discs in pan making sure they do not touch.
6: Put a dab of butter and a sprinkle of salt on each disc.
7: Roast for 25-30 minutes until golden and crispy.
8: Sprinkle with cheese and rosemary and return to the oven for 5 minutes, until melted.
9: Serve.

Riding the Wake. Gliding effortlessly along the wall, this water-skier echoes a rich legacy of lake life that has long defined Winter Haven. A tribute to the area's storied past, this mural captures the spirit of adventure that has drawn both locals and legends to these waters for generations.

Working at the Water's Edge

ECHOES OF LABOR

Tracks stretch their spines across the canal,
Carrying the weight of steel and morning fog.
Freight cars groan with the burden of distance,
And the warehouses stand like old men,
Their faces scarred with years of heavy hands.
Engines murmur to the dawn,
Blending with the cranes' low calls,
And the hum of motors as the fishermen arrive.
The docks creak beneath boots and barrels,
As nets are thrown, and sweat meets water.
The sun rises slow, burning off the mist,
Revealing the ghosts of yesterday's catch,
And the marks left by ropes on wood.
This is where labor meets the lake,
Where hands pull from the water,
And time presses forward with each new haul.
The lakes wear this work like a scar—
A history written in rust, in salt,
And in the quiet strength of those who call this place home.

Chapter Page: Freight Over the Flow. As the train rumbles overhead, a fishing boat slips quietly through the canal below. It's a meeting of two worlds—industry and recreation—where the rhythm of rail and water collide in a scene that speaks to the diverse life of Winter Haven's waterways.

Photo Page: Delivery by the Lake. With the lake shimmering in the background, this FedEx truck seems to pause before the next stop. A quiet moment of stillness, where the rhythm of daily life meets the timeless calm of the water, offering a brief respite before the road calls again.

FedEx
Ground

The lakes of Winter Haven have always been more than just reflections of the sky or serene places for fishing and boating. They have been the lifeblood of a city, shaping the rhythms of work, growth, and progress. In the early days, the canals linking these lakes weren't just pathways for leisure but vital arteries for commerce. Long before the hum of modern engines filled the air, these waters carried the ambitions of the town's early settlers—farmers, laborers, and dreamers. Small boats would ferry crates of citrus from groves lining the shores, and steamboats cut through the misty mornings, their wakes dissolving into the glassy surface. These waterways became Winter Haven's first highways, bearing the weight of a harvest that would define the town's prosperity.

As the 20th century dawned, the arrival of the railroad redefined the city's landscape and its connection to the water. Steel rails stretched over the lakes, forming bridges that spanned the distance between groves and distant markets. The sounds of engines mixed with the whisper of waves as workers loaded railcars with citrus—golden orbs destined for tables far beyond Florida's borders. The packing houses that lined the lakes bustled with activity, their walls echoing with the clatter of machinery and the voices of those whose hands packed, sorted, and moved the lifeblood of the town. The lakes watched silently as trains rumbled across their surface, a partnership between industry and nature that propelled Winter Haven forward.

Even as industry expanded, the lakes remained a constant presence. Warehouses and processing plants rose along the shores, their silhouettes mirrored in the water below. The docks that once saw crates of fruit now served as landing places for rail shipments, and the canals continued to facilitate the flow of goods and dreams. For the workers who moved through these spaces, the rhythm of labor was marked by the pulse of the lakes—steadily beating against the shore.

With time, the nature of work began to change. The citrus industry, so central to Winter Haven's identity, faced challenges—from freezes to shifts in market demands—that forced the town to adapt. As agriculture waned, the opening of Cypress Gardens in the 1930s signaled a new era of tourism. The lakes, once crisscrossed by steamships and cargo boats, now drew visitors eager to experience their beauty. The water that had carried oranges to market now carry jungle cruisers, and the banks that had once supported warehouses now hosted picnic tables and families seeking respite under the cypress trees.

Today, traces of that industrial past linger in the old rail bridges and warehouses, some repurposed as shops, galleries, or restaurants that breathe new life into the structures where citrus once reigned. Yet the lakes remain at the heart of it all, supporting a different kind of work—boat tours that guide visitors through the Chain of Lakes, fishing guides who share the secrets of their waters, and lakeside businesses that continue to draw life from their proximity to the water. The cranes and steam engines have given way to paddleboards and kayaks, but the connection between Winter Haven's labor and its lakes endures.

Generations of workers have come and gone, their stories etched into the shores and the rusted rails that cross the water. The lakes have witnessed it all—the bustling warehouses, the quiet mornings when the fog lifts off the water, and the laughter of children on summer afternoons. They remain, as they always have, a reflection of the city's spirit—a reminder that the story of work in Winter Haven has always been one that flows alongside the water, adapting with the currents of time.

Winter Haven's lakes continue to shape the rhythm of life here, as they did when workers first hauled crates from the groves to the railcars, as they do now when boaters glide across their surface, and as they will in the years to come. They hold the stories of those who toiled at their edges, those who built a city from the water up, and those who find new ways to thrive, always looking to the lakes for inspiration. At the water's edge, where industry and nature meet, Winter Haven's history is still being written, carried forward by the gentle waves that touch its shores.

End of an Era. Behind the "For Sale" sign, the remnants of what once was an industrial lakeside property linger in the sun. The empty lot, framed by palm trees and water, hints at a past filled with activity, now waiting for a new chapter to be written on its shores.

DAVID'S CATCH OF THE DAY

Ingredients:

- Fresh bass fillets (adjust ingredients based on the number of fillets)
- Water (enough to submerge the fillets)
- Juice of 2 lemons
- Salt (to taste)
- 1 cup buttermilk
- 1 egg
- Pepper (to taste)
- ½ cup flour
- ½ cup breadcrumbs
- Vegetable oil (for frying)

Instructions

1: In a large bowl, prepare a brine with water, lemon juice, and a generous pinch of salt. Submerge the fillets in the brine and refrigerate overnight.

2: The next day, remove the fillets from the brine, rinse, and pat them dry with paper towels. In a separate bowl, mix buttermilk, egg, salt, and pepper to taste. Place the fillets into this mixture, ensuring they are fully coated. Cover and refrigerate for 6-8 hours.

3: Remove the fillets from the buttermilk mixture and dip them into the flour and bread crumb mixture, pressing lightly to ensure an even coating.

4: Place the breaded fillets on a cookie sheet and refrigerate for at least 1 hour before frying.

5: Heat vegetable oil to 350°F in a deep pan or fryer. Fry the fillets for about 4 minutes, or until golden brown and crispy.

6: Remove from the oil and drain on a paper towel. Serve hot, with your favorite sides.

Lakeside Industry. In the shadow of towering dairy tanks, a quiet boat rests by the water's edge. Here, the past and present of Winter Haven's industrial heart sit side by side—where the serenity of the lake contrasts with the hum of production, reminding us of the delicate balance between nature and industry.

Enduring Strength

TO WHAT IS STILL TO COME

The lakes are connection,
A link that binds us to this place,
Where the cypress roots dig deep,
And we find ourselves grounded
In their enduring strength.
They reach across time,
They reach beyond memory,
They reach for what is yet to come,
A bridge between what was
And what will be.
Here, the water holds our stories,
Each ripple a promise,
Each wave a whisper of what is still to come.
And when the sun sinks low,
Dipping its light beneath the surface,
We stand at the edge,
Looking out at the sky's mirrored face,
Knowing that some part of us remains—
Held in the currents,
Carried forward to tomorrow.

Chapter Page: Evening Reflection. As the sun dips below the horizon, the lake becomes a mirror, reflecting the fading light. Framed by the silhouette of the cypress tree, the scene offers a quiet moment of stillness—where nature's beauty is captured in the peaceful transition from day to night.

Photo Page: Summit Sentinels. Standing tall and unyielding, these cypress trees are guardians of the lake, rooted deeply in the past while watching over the future. Their strength, tested by time and storm, reflects a quiet resilience—ensuring that what they protect will endure for generations to come.

The lakes of Winter Haven, with their gentle currents and quiet expanses, have always held a kind of timelessness. They have been here long before roads crisscrossed the land, before the engines of boats and trains echoed over the water, before the cypress trees stretched their roots deep into the lakebed. And they will remain, long after we have added our stories to the ripples. These lakes are not just bodies of water; they are memory itself, a reflection of the people who have lived, worked, and played along their shores.

The cypress trees that line the lakes have witnessed it all. Their roots dig deep into the dark soil, holding fast through every storm, bending but never breaking. Like the people who have built their lives here, these trees endure. They have stood through the years of abundance and the times of struggle, through the calm and the chaos, absorbing each season's lessons. Their branches stretch out over the water, casting shadows that shift with the sun, always reaching towards what is yet to come.

The lakes hold these stories, too—stories of steamboats that once cut through the misty mornings, of citrus crates and freight trains, of children daring the waves in summer's heat. Even now, as modern life pulses around them, the lakes keep their secrets. They remember the early settlers who saw opportunity in their waters, the generations who found both work and rest at their edges. Each ripple is a reminder of those who have come before, and the water carries these memories forward, like echoes drifting on a breeze.

In a place where time seems to move differently, the lakes become a mirror, reflecting not just the sky above but the lives of those who stand at their shores. In the quiet of a morning spent fishing or a sunset shared from a dock, the water offers a space to remember, to pause, to feel connected to something larger. It is here, in these moments, that the lakes remind us of the endurance found in stillness, in the way they hold each story gently beneath the surface, waiting to be remembered.

Yet, the lakes are not just about looking back. They have always pointed forward, their waters a promise that there is still more to come. They continue to be a place where new stories are written—where families gather for picnics beneath the cypress trees, where children learn to swim, where friends tie up boats to share a meal on the water.

The lakes offer a sense of continuity, a reminder that even as the world changes around us, some things remain constant.The lakes offer a sense of continuity, a reminder that even as the world changes around us, some things remain constant.

The strength of the lakes is not in their resistance to change but in their ability to hold everything—past, present, and future—within their depths. They have seen the town grow and adapt, seen industries rise and fade, seen communities weather the storms and come together in the calm that follows. They endure, just as the people of Winter Haven endure, finding resilience in their connection to these waters.

As we look out over the lakes, watching the sun dip beneath the horizon, it's easy to feel a sense of hope. The lakes have carried us this far, through seasons of growth and change, through times when the water seemed uncertain and times when it was as steady as our own heartbeat. They will continue to carry us, reminding us that there is strength in staying true to our roots, in bending without breaking, in holding onto the things that matter even as time moves on.

And so, the lakes will remain, just as they always have—mirroring the sky, holding the echoes of our laughter and our losses, and flowing steadily into what is still to come. They remind us that while everything else may change, the connection we share with this place, with each other, and with the water that surrounds us, is what truly endures. Here, at the water's edge, we find the strength to carry on, knowing that some part of us will always remain, cradled in the currents, carried forward into tomorrow.

Of course, living here requires more than just quiet reflection. It means learning to coexist with a landscape that's as unpredictable as it is beautiful. There's something uniquely Floridian about marveling at the serenity of the lakes while keeping one eye out for a gator lurking just beneath the surface. The cypress trees may be unyielding, but the mosquitoes? They're relentless. The water offers a cool escape, but let's not forget the hurricanes that remind us just how fragile even the strongest roots can be. Living here is a lesson in resilience—learning to appreciate the beauty while respecting the wildness, knowing that this place, stronger than us, sometimes seems determined to outlast and outwit us.

But maybe that's part of why we love it so much. There's an irony in knowing that the lakes, with their peaceful veneer, can also be fierce and untamable. They're a reminder that the natural world has its own rules and timelines, and we're just lucky to be along for the ride. After all, what's a little unpredictability if it means living in a place where nature constantly challenges us—and where, every once in a while, we, as Florida Lake People rise to meet it?

Milton's Casting Couch. The red stapler survived in this lakefront office, but the couch didn't. Now it is waiting for its next pickup that, just like that paycheck, might never come.

PASSION FRUIT TART

Ingredients:

- 1 pre-baked tart shell (9-inch)
- 1 cup passion fruit puree
- 1/2 cup sugar
- 4 egg yolks
- 1/2 cup unsalted butter, cubed

Instructions

1: In a saucepan, combine passion fruit puree, sugar, and egg yolks over medium heat.
2: Stir continuously until the mixture thickens, about 5-7 minutes.
3: Remove from heat and whisk in butter until smooth.
4: Pour the warm mixture into the pre-baked tart shell.
5: Chill in the refrigerator for at least 2 hours before serving.

Resilience Unfurled. As the storm passed, the flag at Twisted Prop remained steadfast, a symbol of endurance against the odds. Framed by the calm waters and the glowing shoreline, it stands tall—just like the people of this town—ready to rebuild and carry on. The strength of the lakes, the community, and the land remains, unwavering through the trials of time.

ABOUT THE AUTHOR

The author and artist Amanda McCallister was born at Winter Haven Hospital to David and Doris McCallister. She grew up on the chain of lakes with her Grandfather Fred Wright as her guide to lake front living. She graduated from Winter Haven High School and went on to Stetson University where she majored in English. While at Stetson she met her husband, Thomas Lentz. Upon graduation, she taught at her Alma Matters Westwood Middle School, then Winter Haven High School, before helping to open Ridge Community High School with her professional mentor Sherry Trent Wells. While at Ridge, she rediscovered her love of artwork while founding and sponsoring a student leadership organization, Sigma Alpha Sigma, which required her to design and create extensive craft projects for student recognitions, decorations for events, and graphic designs for marketing. She earned her master's degree in education from the American College of Education during her more than a decade as an educator. She would later go on to work for the Lake Wales Public Library and Lake Wales Arts Council. Her career as an artist took off during this time with her works being featured in galleries throughout central Florida and a stint exhibiting at outdoor art shows. She is currently a full-time entrepreneur. This book fulfills one of her lifelong goals to be a published author.

www.ingramcontent.com/pod-product-compliance
Ingram Content Group UK Ltd.
Pitfield, Milton Keynes, MK11 3LW, UK
UKHW060324060826
14089UKWH00005BA/79

9 798330 556014